COPYRIGHT

ISBN-13: 978-0-692-50760-5

Published by
Kimberly Wells
PO Box 61
Worthing, SD 57077
USA

ACKNOWLEDGEMENTS

For many years, I have been encouraged by friends and relatives to write a book as I've had many challenging, character-building and sometimes traumatic experiences in my life. I wasn't moved to publish anything until the events that occurred as detailed in this book, Losing Mason. I would like to acknowledge those people who have encouraged and supported my writing:

First: Mason, who inspired me to tell about his brief life. We are changed as a result of his passing and I do not want him to be forgotten.

The Lord: Without my relationship with Him, I would not have had the strength to continue and to write this book.

My mom: Patricia Gildemeister for her love, support and encouragement.

My husband: Daniel Wells, who had faith in my talents, abilities and who believed in me even when I didn't.

My uncle: Michael Tidemann for being the copy editor for this book and for being my mentor.

My friend: JD Simone for being my editor.

My foster mom: Elizabeth Bowling, for her love, support, and encouragement and who also created the beautiful book cover.

My sister Stephanie and my sweet friends who supported me throughout this difficult time: Becca, Lori, Marti and Vicki.

Finally, my children, who have given me strength, encouragement and inspiration to continue through life, you are my most precious blessings!

DEDICATION

This book is dedicated to my eldest son, Jesse Warren Lokken, his former girlfriend, Yvette Jeunesse, and my late grandson, Mason Warren Lokken. What was supposed to be a time of joyous celebration instead turned into one of profound grief when we lost Mason on December 14, 2013. The healing process, while harder than I ever thought possible, drew us closer together as a family and taught me that we are all much stronger than we ever could have imagined. I know my strength came from the Lord. There is no way I could have made it through this without him.

The strength, courage, and love exhibited between Jesse and Yvette during this tragic and heart-breaking loss was extraordinary. I have never been so proud of the both of them in the way they conducted themselves and comforted each other during this most difficult time.

Although he didn't get to take a breath in this life, Mason's very existence has touched our hearts and our lives forever. Mason is our angel in Heaven now and we can't wait until the day comes when we can all be with him, together again! We love you little man: We will see you in paradise!

TABLE OF CONTENTS

CHAPTER ONE

My oldest son Jesse and his girlfriend Yvette were expecting a baby, and I was eagerly awaiting the birth of my second grandchild. After the multiple losses and heartache I'd endured over the past several years, it was a welcome change to have something to look forward to. As if things weren't difficult enough due to my husband Dan's fight against Non-Hodgkin's Lymphoma, I'd lost my dear sweet grandmother, Margaret Tidemann, to cancer, and my best friend Val to recurrence of breast cancer. It was a rough decade or so, but a constant light in our blended family was our children, his, mine and ours. Both Dan and I have two children from previous marriages, Jim and Sarah from Dan's, and Jesse and Brandy from mine. And then we have Brian, our only child together. Born with Down syndrome, he's one of the sweetest, most lovable children you'll ever meet. Jesse had previously blessed us with our only grandchild, and our first grandson, Brendan, now eleven years old. But the birth of a new grandbaby couldn't have come at a better time. It was a very exciting time.

Jesse and Yvette hadn't planned the pregnancy, but they were both making steps to prepare and make sure they were ready to take care of their little bundle of joy. Every time we talked about their baby they both beamed. It was evident that they were both happy and joyful and they were looking forward to being parents.

Jesse continued to work while Yvette was nesting and they made room in their apartment for a nursery and began to prepare for their baby's arrival.

I sorted through some of the baby stuff that I had kept from Brian and I had two tubs of baby items for them.

We talked about baby nursery themes and items they would need to have before the baby was born.

Yvette was attending her doctor appointments and she was taking care of herself. She had not encountered any problems until the end of her pregnancy when she was diagnosed with gestational diabetes, which was being closely monitored by her physician.

Both Jesse and Yvette would call me every once in a while and ask my opinion about various baby names that they were considering. They found out they were having a boy, and I was honored that they shared their thoughts and ideas with me regarding the potential name of my new grandson. I felt really involved and I was excited in the anticipation of having another grandchild. After careful consideration, Jesse and Yvette finally chose their new baby boy's name, Mason Warren. I was very proud and honored that they had chosen that name as I had named Jesse, Jesse Warren. Jesse's middle name Warren was chosen as it was his father's middle name. It had a lot of significance and I knew it would mean a lot to Jesse's father, my ex-husband, Richard. I saw the look on Rich's face when Jesse told him what name they had decided for our new grandson. I could tell that Rich was surprised and gleamed with pride.

Rich, his wife, Sharon, my husband Dan and I wanted to make sure that Jesse and Yvette had everything they needed for our new grandson so we purchased a crib with a changing table, crib sheets, crib bumper pads, blankets, and a crib mobile all in a Cars theme. We also bought a bassinet and baby clothes. Together with items from other family members and friends, they had everything they needed for their baby's arrival.

Jesse & Yvette at their baby shower.

My daughter Brandy made a diaper cake for the baby shower, which didn't happen as we had planned, but instead we held a family baby shower after our Thanksgiving dinner, at our home. For the shower, we also had a beautiful cake with our grandson's name on it - green sherbet punch with a mom and two baby rubber ducks floating on top of the punch in the punch bowl and bountiful gifts.

It was awesome to watch them open and view their gifts for their baby boy. They were both so happy and glowing knowing that they had everything they needed to provide for the birth of their son.

It had been nine years since I experienced the joy of having a grandchild and I too was happy and excited. I hadn't realized it until much later, but it was actually the only event that I had been looking forward to for many years.

It was evident after the baby shower that both Jesse and Yvette felt ready and excited for their son to enter this world.

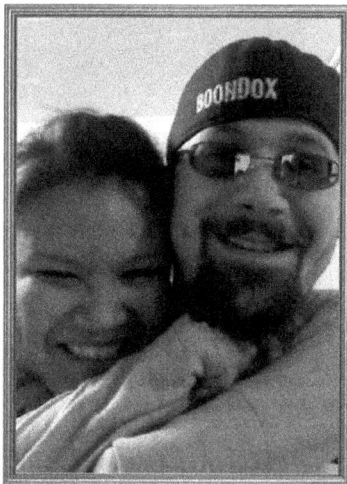

One of my favorite pictures of Jesse & Yvette together as they looked so happy.

Jesse and Yvette had sent me pictures of my new grandson's ultrasounds and I shared in their excitement. The closer Yvette was to her due date, the more excited and anxious we had all become.

I had already asked my mom if I could get my grandfather's baby cradle that was handcrafted by my great-grandfather, so that I would have it at my home for whenever Mason would be at Grandma's house.

As Yvette's pregnancy progressed the anticipation increased and I was so thrilled to have another grandchild entering this world. It became a bright light in my life and it gave me something amazing to look forward to. Being a mother was awesome, but being a grandmother was even better.

I was so looking forward to having another grandchild. I had imagined cradling and cuddling my new grandson and thinking about all the time I would be able to spend with him; play with him; teach him about our traditions; and watch him grow up into a big, tall, strong, handsome, and loving young man.

CHAPTER TWO

It was on December 14, 2013, eleven days before Christmas, and earlier in the day I was on my way to a fundraiser for my friend Dale's wife, who had been diagnosed with breast cancer. I had been traveling down a major street in Sioux Falls and I saw this young couple trudging through the snow-covered sidewalks and at one point, the young man set the groceries down on the sidewalk and you could tell they were both cold and struggling. I turned my van around and pulled up beside them, turned my flashers on, and I asked them if they needed a ride. I could tell that they were shocked that someone actually stopped and offered them a ride. They both climbed into the back of my van with their groceries. The young man said, "Where I come from, no one would ever stop and offer someone a ride". I asked him where he was from. He said that he was from Florida and his girlfriend was from Sioux Falls. They had just moved here a few weeks ago to try and start a new life and they were looking for work. I told them that I felt that God wanted me to stop and give them a ride as they looked like they were struggling and cold and they needed help. They kind of looked at me weird, but I was ok with it as that is what happened. They lived a little over a mile from where I picked them up. Once we arrived at their apartment building, they got out of my van with their groceries in tow and they were so grateful. I smiled and I told them to, "pay it forward", and I drove away and continued on my way to my friend's wife's benefit.

When I arrived at the benefit that was being held at the Knights of Columbus in Sioux Falls, S.D., a dear friend of mine, Marti, was waiting for me. We sat together with another friend of Marti's and her family members and we enjoyed bidding on the silent auction items. We bought t-shirts and we had lunch.

We also had a chance to talk to our friend Dale. Marti and I told Dale that we were here if he needed anything and he told us he knew that we would be.

I had also brought some items for the bake sale. They were cakes made from scratch. It was actually the first time I was able to get out of the house for a while and relax. It felt great to be out and to be around a few friends. I needed the break.

After the benefit I returned home for the day and I made my husband Dan and my son, Brian, some dinner.

Later that evening, I was driving to Sioux Falls, S.D., to pick up my sister Stephanie who was here visiting from Washington State. She extended her stay to a few weeks so that she could spend time with her father, my stepfather, Harvey, as his health was ailing.

That evening, Stephanie had been visiting Harvey who was admitted to Sanford USD Medical Center, a local hospital. Harvey had been readmitted to the hospital three times in two weeks and he didn't seem to recover each time and he was definitely losing ground. We had been told earlier in the week that we should consider whether Harvey should return to the nursing home or consider moving him to hospice. After a discussion with many of the different medical providers, my sister, Stephanie, my brother, Mark, and my aunt Helen and I, we decided that Harvey would get better care at the hospice due to the nurse/technician-to-patient ratio. Since it was evident that he would receive better care there than he had been at the nursing home, where he had been residing for the last twenty-six months that is where we decided Harvey was going to be transferred upon his discharge from the hospital.

Stephanie and I had made plans for the night to go out for dinner with our Mom, her boyfriend Jim, and our uncle Mike, who had been visiting from Iowa, and maybe get out for a little while for one last hoorah until the next time we would see each other again. While I was on my way to the hospital to pick up my sister for dinner, I received a text message from Yvette.

As Yvette was getting further along and she was approaching her due date, her doctor appointments increased and the doctor she had chosen practiced in a clinic in Sioux Falls. During the last couple of weeks Yvette had remained with her grandmother so that she would be able to get to her doctor appointments and she would be in Sioux Falls when she went in to labor.

Yvette's original due date was January 4, 2014, but her due date had been moved up to December 24, 2013. Jesse was a Christmas baby and he was born on December 22nd, so I was hoping that maybe Mason would be born on his birthday.

Yvette's text message said that she was on the way to Sanford USD Medical Center, as she had not felt her baby Mason move all day and her doctor told her to go to the emergency room. She was over eight months along, ten days from her due date. I arrived at the emergency room before Yvette and eagerly waited in the emergency room lobby until she arrived.

Yvette's father had driven her to the hospital and he dropped Yvette off at the emergency room. Yvette came in to the lobby and I was surprised that she was by herself. I asked Yvette where her dad was and she told me that she and her father had gotten into a disagreement about the name she had chosen for her baby. He wanted Mason to have the same last name as he and Yvette...

After completing the paperwork, we were taken to the triage room in the labor and delivery section of the hospital. Yvette told me that the night before she was woken out of a deep sleep with a sharp stabbing pain. It made her wonder if that is when something happened.

The doctor ordered an ultrasound. The technician hooked up the electrodes to Yvette in various places. Yvette told me that Mason had not been moving at all and she was concerned and afraid.

I was with Yvette while the procedure was performed and I watched the screen, hoping to see that everything was ok.

The technician continued to wand Yvette's pregnant belly in different areas, trying to locate the baby's heartbeat. At one point we thought we had heard his heartbeat but it was Yvette's, not Masons. I closed my eyes and prayed that I would hear my baby grandson's heart beating... I did not.

I looked up towards the ceiling and said, "Really, this can't be happening right now". How could God let this happen?

CHAPTER THREE

My ex-husband, Rich, Jesse's dad, lives in the same town as our son, Jesse, in Mitchell, SD, which is approximately 70 miles away from the hospital. I told Rich that Yvette was at the hospital and she had not felt the baby move all day. I requested that he go to our son's house and pick him up and bring him to the hospital in Sioux Falls.

I sent my sister Stephanie a text to let her know that we couldn't find the baby's heartbeat and that I was with Yvette at the same hospital where my step-dad was also being treated. Next thing I knew, Stephanie was there outside Yvette's room. At first, I didn't even recognize her. In shock, dazed and completely lost, it took me a while to recognize my own sister.

Stephanie and I went back into Yvette's room and we tried to comfort her while we waited for Yvette's family to arrive and for her doctor to decide what we needed to do next. Yvette was crushed. We all three sat there together with Stephanie and I holding Yvette's hands, while we sobbed.

We were informed that Yvette's doctor requested a more thorough ultrasound. My sister asked what she should do, and I told her to go back to our dad's hospital room, on the other side of the hospital, so she could spend more time with him before she had to say good-bye. She was returning home to Tacoma, Washington the following day. She thought this would be the last time she would see our father alive.

I went with Yvette to the second ultrasound. A technician was called in to the hospital to complete the examination from Mason's feet to his head. I tried to comfort Yvette and I prayed that we would hear my grandson's heartbeat.

Again, I watched the screen and listened intently, while the technician moved slowly with the ultrasound device and we waited anxiously, hoping that he was just turned around and that is why they couldn't hear his heart beating.

Yvette and I were bawling and she couldn't bear to view the ultrasound screen. She rested her head back against the pillow on the bed. She was so sad and scared, while tears were streaming down both of our faces.

As the technician continued the scan with the ultrasound wand upward, I watched on the screen, which indicated what area was being scanned. I had seen the scan had reached baby Mason's chest and the technician began to take images. I could see his heart, but it wasn't beating...

In between the scan of Mason's chest and his head, I saw a horizontal line. I thought oh, my God, could this really be happening, was he really gone, is that the umbilical cord? I couldn't bear to tell Yvette, as I didn't know if that is what I was seeing or not. I held her hand, rubbed her arm and shoulder and a river of tears burst. We were scared, shocked beyond belief, and completely devastated.

This had NEVER even entered our minds... It was unthinkable.

CHAPTER FOUR

Yvette is a Lakota Sioux Native American, and she is a member of the Crow Creek Reservation. She was raised by her grandmother Yvonne, her dad's mother. Yvette acquired the nickname "baby girl" early in life in order to minimize the confusion when her aunt Yvette, her namesake, was around.

I wasn't sure what was customary in Native American culture when something like this occurred, but I did know that Yvette needed all the support that she could possibly have and I also knew she was very close to her family, especially her dad and her grandmother.

I called Yvette's aunt and told her that I was with Yvette at the hospital, and that after two ultrasounds the doctor was unable to find Mason's heartbeat. Yvette's aunt sounded as though she was stunned and devastated. I asked her to get a hold of Yvette's father and grandmother and have them come up to the hospital as Yvette desperately needed them both. She said she would pick up Yvette's grandmother and bring her up to the hospital.

I went back to Yvette's triage room in the labor and delivery area and I tried to comfort her, but I didn't know what to say other than I was so sorry. At one point, I caught myself almost uttering it would be ok, but I stopped myself as I knew it wouldn't be. I hugged her, tried to comfort her, and I cried with her while we waited for her family members to arrive.

Once Yvette's grandmother, her aunt, her cousin Nate and his girlfriend Kristeen arrived, I stepped outside to let her have time alone with her family. Her family took turns visiting with her. I called my mom and told her what had happened and I sobbed and sobbed. I felt a wrenching pain, deep in my gut and I felt light-headed, dazed, and nauseous. I stepped outside to feel some brisk, fresh, cold air to help calm myself down. I stood outside of the hospital and called my ex-husband to see how far they were away from the hospital.

I provided Rich and Jesse with an update on Yvette and the baby. I stood outside by the bench in the brisk cold evening, with tears rolling down my face. I couldn't stop crying. I returned to the entrance of the hospital and I cried all the way through the lobby and back to the hospital waiting room where some of Yvette's relatives were waiting to see her.

Yvette told me she needed Jesse and she couldn't get through this without him. Once Jesse arrived, he came into the room, sat down on the side of Yvette's hospital bed, and they clutched on to each other, embraced and cried uncontrollably. She did so need him. She was right. I really don't think she would have been able to make it through this loss without him.

Watching Jesse and Yvette suffering in pain over the devastating loss of their son Mason was painful and heart wrenching.

CHAPTER FIVE

One of the hospital personnel put a dragonfly on Yvette's hospital room door. The hospital staff explained to Jesse and Yvette that they place the dragonfly on the hospital room doors of parents whose babies have passed away; that way the hospital staff is aware of their loss. They gave them a pamphlet called Dragonfly Story together with some other material. The story uses a colony of water bugs to explain the circle of life. Every once in a while a water bug would climb up a lily stalk and never come back, and the others would wonder where he went. Finally one of the water bugs said that he had an idea. The next water bug who climbs up the lily stalk must promise to come back and tell everyone where he or she went and why. One day a water bug climbed up the stalk, and before he knew what was happening, he had broken through the surface of the water and fallen onto a lily pad. He turned into a dragonfly before he could get back down and tell the others. He realized he would have to wait until the rest of the water bugs became dragonflies before he could tell them and before they would understand what happened to him and where he went.

Although the story was created to explain death to young children, I found it to be a very touching, sweet story regarding remembering your loved ones who have passed away and to remind you that you will one day be with them again.

The hospital also gave them a wooden keepsake box with a dragonfly on the cover, which was for their mementos of Mason. Yvette had various things enclosed in her keepsake box including a portion of Mason's umbilical cord.

We reviewed some of the material they provided. We sat in Yvette's hospital room in silence, shock and reeling from the news, the reality. It seemed surreal, unbelievable, frightening, earth shattering and for some time it shook my foundation. What we thought was to be the future and the direction our family was headed had collapsed. We felt sad, angry, shocked, confused, and completely lost.

Jesse had left home so quickly when he came to Sioux Falls, he didn't think to bring any extra clothes. I did some clothes shopping for him, and purchased some toiletries. I also bought Yvette some furry slippers and a super-soft blanket and pillow. I thought that they may be soothing and provide her with some comfort while she was in the hospital. I brought them over to the hospital, and then I showed Jesse where the nutrition center was so he could get a snack or something to drink when he wanted.

The doctor came to the hospital room later that evening and she notified Yvette that they would have to induce her labor as when she arrived at the hospital she was not dilated. Mason had passed away, so they had to medically assist her body in an effort to deliver him.

The following day, Jesse stayed by Yvette's side. They cuddled, cried, grieved, and we talked. Yvette told me that their family usually uses Miller Funeral Home and they would like the service for Mason's funeral to be held at Calvary Episcopal Cathedral, which is actually located across from the funeral home. We began to discuss their wishes. They decided they wanted a service combining Native American customs with a Christian service.

On the wall in Yvette's hospital room across from her bed was a picture of a woman with her son. One of Yvette's relatives had covered it with the prayer shawl. When I noticed that, I removed the picture from the wall and turned it around and rested the picture against the wall. I removed the prayer shawl and gave it back to Yvette. I didn't think she needed to be subjected to looking at that picture of a woman and her young son, when she was enduring the loss of her baby boy.

At one point, Jesse and I left the hospital room and we went to the parking ramp and sat in my van. We talked about everything and he broke down crying. I hugged him and tears started streaming down our faces. I told Jesse that I was so proud of him for how he was handling this loss and for how he was staying by Yvette's side, staying strong and helping her get through this. My heart hurt witnessing these two in pain.

I knew I couldn't fix it, but I tried to do whatever I could to make them feel better... I just wanted to do what I could for both of them. I couldn't imagine what they were feeling. Mason was my grandson and I knew how bad I felt, but he was their son.

We were walking back to Yvette's room and there were baby pictures on the walls all the way down the hallway and Jesse made a comment about how hard it was to see all the baby pictures when he knew that Mason was gone. I had thought the very same thing earlier that day.

Later that evening, Yvette's father, Lorenzo, arrived at the hospital with Yvette's brother Dakota, and three other men. Lorenzo and Yvette are Lakota Sioux Native American, and the men came to perform a ritual ceremony. Lorenzo had brought Yvette's feather, which he had kept for her since she was a baby.

In doing research about Native American history and culture I learned that Native Americans believe the eagle lives in both worlds; here on heaven and in the spirit world. There are a lot of stories that the Native Americans have told throughout history to show the significance the eagle has to them and their culture. The eagle is a chief bird. The feathers the chief has in his headdress were eagle feathers that he earned. In Native American culture an eagle feather is a symbol. It can symbolize many things including, but not limited to wisdom, freedom, trust, strength, power, and honor. A feather is usually earned in one way or another. It may be given to someone for helping someone else, or it may have been earned through a brave act. Men and women could earn an eagle feather and it was like an award. Once you receive a feather, the feather has to be displayed. It may not be hidden.

It is often hung in a room in a home and it is treated somewhat like the American flag. It has to be taken care of and preserved and it may never touch the ground.

Lorenzo told her that he had kept it and had not given it to her before as he had not felt that she was ready for it. Lorenzo said, "Now baby girl, I believe you have matured, and you are ready". Lorenzo handed Yvette her feather. Lorenzo had also brought a feather for Mason.

Mason's feather was given to Yvette to honor Mason and his death. The two feathers were hung in Yvette's hospital room and her father handed her a peace pipe. A ceremony was performed and it is called Yuwipi, (pronounced yoo-WEE-pee). It is a traditional ceremony of the Lakota people that can be performed any time and it is usually performed to heal a sick or injured person. It can also be used for curing, prophesy and to find lost or missing people or items. Yuwipi is similar to the Sun Dance ceremony as it uses the sacred peace pipe to connect with spirits.

Yvette sat up in her bed holding the peace pipe. The elders said a prayer in native language. Her father started crumbling the white sage to cleanse his wounded daughter. He said they couldn't light the sage in the hospital as it was against hospital rules. I said, "This is a religious ritual, you should be able to burn it". The sage is meant for cleansing and protection. Her father rubbed the sage on Yvette's legs, arms and her hair. Lorenzo said a prayer in native language and then English. He stated that our two families are now one and that we needed prayers, comfort, and peace to get us through this tragic loss.

One of the elders said he had a dream that Mason had been here before and that he saw Yvette and that he wanted her to be his mother. The elder also said that Mason's spirit would be here for four days and then an eagle would take his spirit to heaven. Native Americans believe that there are five different bird spirits. An eagle is considered to be an extremely powerful bird and it would therefore have a powerful spirit as well.

Lorenzo mentioned that he was trying to arrange a sweat in honor of Mason.

A sweat ceremony is a sacred Native American tradition. "Inipi Wakan," in Lakota Sioux and it is one of the oldest rituals in North America. A sweat lodge is a round dome-like structure that is formed by willow tree branches. The dome is covered with a canvas and blankets. The center of the circle has hot lava rocks and the leader of the sweat pours water on the lava stones, which creates, permeates, and immerses the dome with steamy bellowing heat. The dome is dark inside and the sweat continues in twenty- minute increments for four sessions. Sage, tobacco, cedar, and sweet grass may be burned to help balance your body's senses. The inside of the sweat structure heats up, prayers are said, and sacred songs are typically sung. The sweat is used to purify and balance your body. The individuals participating in the sweat form a prayer/healing circle to clean their body, mind, and spirit. Often the use of a sacred pipe, "Chanupa Wakan Cha" in Lakota Sioux, also known as a peace pipe, was used to smoke tobacco wrapped in corn husks. It is believed that the tobacco smoke carries their prayers to Heaven.

My ex-husband Rich and I thanked Yvette's father and the other men that came to attempt to provide some comfort to Yvette and our families. How painful was this mourning; how deep that pain has cut.

The doctor told us that Yvette would not be delivering Mason until the morning so I talked to Jesse and Yvette and told them that I would go home and leave them alone for the night. I asked them to call me if she went in to labor in the middle of the night.

CHAPTER SIX

It was 5:00 a.m. I woke up to my cell phone ringing... It was Jesse calling me from Yvette's cell phone. He told me that the doctor was coming back to the hospital and they were preparing to have Yvette get ready to start pushing to deliver Mason. I climbed out of bed and threw on some sweat pants and I told my husband I was going to the hospital for Mason's birth.

I cried and prayed on the way to the hospital and I asked God to give me the strength to do what I needed to do, which was to be there for Jesse and Yvette at the birth of their son and to hold my grandson Mason after he was delivered.

I arrived at the hospital as fast as I could and when I reached Yvette's hospital room she was prepared for delivery. Her feet were up in the stirrups and she was dilated far enough to start pushing. The doctor and three other medical professionals were in the room and Yvette's grandmother arrived at the hospital shortly thereafter.

Jesse, Yvette's grandmother, and I were present when Mason was delivered. The umbilical cord was wrapped around his neck, but it was not tight. I wondered why he had to be gone. What happened?

CHAPTER SEVEN

It was heart-wrenching to see Yvette having to deliver her baby knowing that he had already passed away. As Mason's grandmother I was feeling pain like nothing I had felt before. I couldn't imagine what Yvette and Jesse were going through. I just kept praying we would all make it through this and that we would all have the strength to do what we needed to do. Mason was born at 6:08 a.m. on Monday, December 16, 2013. He weighed 7 lbs. 14 oz., and was 21-1/2" long.

Mason was laid on Yvette's tummy after the delivery and she cuddled him, stroked his back, and looked into his beautiful face. Our hearts all broke as we experienced this enormous, tragic, unimaginable loss of such a beautiful, healthy-looking baby boy. Our dreams of the life we thought we were going to have with this glorious baby were immediately crushed.

I held Mason after Yvette and Jesse had held him. I cuddled him in my arms and gazed at his beautiful face and I said The Lord's Prayer. I remember looking at my son Jesse and thinking "WHY", he was perfect, why was such a beautiful baby gone? I kissed my grandson Mason's forehead and handed him to Yvette's grandmother, Yvonne. She held Mason while I read Psalm 23 with tears flowing from my eyes to the point that I could barely see. I then tried to comfort Yvette's grandmother while she held Mason, by putting my hand on her shoulder, as she looked into Mason's face and cried. Jesse and Yvette comforted each other, embracing each other and sobbing. We all sat together in Yvette's hospital room in complete devastation and shock. We all wondered WHY? He was so big and healthy and beautiful. How could this have happened?

Yvette's grandmother left the hospital and returned home to rest. I stayed at the hospital until around 9:30 a.m. and I left Jesse and Yvette alone to be with Mason.

Another part of the Lakota tradition is to put food out for the spirits to receive nourishment after a person passes away. Yvette's father reminded Yvette to do this before he left the hospital. Yvette abided by this ritual and she put out a plate with bread for nourishment, which stayed there until we left the hospital.

CHAPTER EIGHT

I left Yvette's hospital room sobbing and I walked through the hallway, skywalk and into the parking lot with tears rolling down my face, wailing...

I found my Dodge Grand Caravan and as soon as I calmed down a little, I left and I drove to Miller Funeral Home. I tried to remain focused while driving and my thoughts began to flood with everything that had happened and everything that needed to be done.

In my college days, I worked as a waitress at a bakery in Sioux Falls called Phillips Avenue Bakery. One of my regular customers was a funeral director for Miller Funeral Home.

I arrived at the funeral home and asked for this former customer, Tim Wingen. He came out of his office into the entry way and we sat down and I tried to refresh his memory as to how we had previously met. He remembered me from the bakery and he knew my aunt Helen and my step-dad, Harvey, as a result of prior family funerals that were held at the funeral home. I told Mr. Wingen about the passing of my grandson Mason. He was very thoughtful, caring, and compassionate. I explained to him that neither Jesse nor Yvette had the funds to pay for Mason's proper burial and that I was now self-employed and my husband had recently been declared disabled. We weren't in a position to pay for a funeral. He told me that they do not charge families for the funeral expenses for infants. It felt as though an enormous weight had been lifted from my shoulders. Mr. Wingen also told me about an organization, the Angel Lee Cronen Memorial Fund. They provide the cost for the coffins for the loss of an infant or child. In some cases, they will pay for other additional expenses such as a headstone or grave marker for the baby's grave.

After I was done talking to Mr. Wingen, I thanked him for his assistance and I told him that he had already provided our family with significant relief due to providing our family with the means for a decent burial for my grandson. I also thanked him for their compassion and generosity. Mr. Wingen directed me to Woodlawn Cemetery as they often donate burial plots to a family who has lost an infant or a child.

At Woodlawn Cemetery, I talked to Kris Howard, the manager, and informed her that I was referred to her by Mr. Tim Wingen of Miller Funeral Home. I explained that my grandson was born stillborn earlier that day and I was told that occasionally they donate plots for infants and children. Kris was compassionate. She listened intently, and she consoled me after I told her of my grandson's passing. Kris gave me a map of the cemetery with the directions to the section where babies and infants are laid to rest, the "Evergreen" section. Kris also informed me that they would be willing to donate the plot, but we would be required to pay for the exhumation of the gravesite. I thanked her for the donation of Mason's plot and I told her how helpful they have all been and that I found their compassion and direction was providing us with some relief and comfort. Kris suggested I check with the church to make sure we could hold the service on the day we wanted.

I drove to the Evergreen section to see where all the little angels are laid to rest. It was an easy section to locate in a cemetery that can be a little confusing at times because of all of the different sections, curves and angles of the grounds construction. We have other family members and friends buried in that cemetery and this is where my husband and I plan to be laid to rest with Brian beside us eventually. It felt like it was the right place for Mason to be now that he was gone.

I left the cemetery and drove to Calvary Episcopal Cathedral and I met with the Dean, the Very Reverend Ward Simpson. He too was caring and compassionate regarding our family's loss and he had been to the hospital earlier in the day to visit with Jesse and Yvette. The Dean knew Yvette's family as they attended his church. He confirmed that we could have a wake for Mason on Wednesday and a funeral on Thursday, with the burial following the funeral at Woodlawn Cemetery and a luncheon back at the church after Mason's burial. I asked the Dean if he would say a prayer for me and give me strength to get through the next few days. He so graciously did pray for me and my family.

I called Woodlawn and told Kris of the arrangements we were making for Mason so that everything would be coordinated. I scheduled an appointment for Jesse and Yvette to meet with the funeral director at the funeral home upon her release from the hospital the next day.

The hospital staff talked to Jesse and Yvette regarding whether they wanted Mason's hand and foot prints and molds prepared for them and they said that they did. The staff came in and got Mason so they could be completed. After they were done, Mason was brought back so Jesse and Yvette could reluctantly say their good-byes before he was transferred to the funeral home.

Jesse and Yvette received a set of Mason's hand and foot prints and molds of Mason's hands and feet.

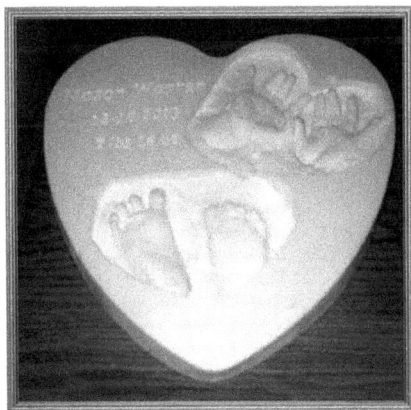

For those few days, I went back and forth between Harvey's hospital room and Yvette's hospital room. They were on the opposite sides of the hospital. I would check on my step-dad, visit with him for a while, finalized his paperwork for the hospice he was being transferred to and maintained a presence near Jesse, and Yvette so that I would be there if they needed me.

It helped to stay busy during these days, focusing on what needed to be done for my husband, my son Brian, my dad, my son Jesse, and Yvette. I received that advice from a couple of people and it certainly helped get me through those initial days. I felt like I was a robot in the "on" position, tackling one task, problem, or issue at a time. It seemed like when I wasn't busy and I had too much time to think the emotions and feelings of despair crept up and I felt like I couldn't stay in that realm for long. I had to keep moving. I had to keep putting one foot in front of the other. I knew deep down in my heart Mason would want me to.

CHAPTER NINE

Harvey was supposed to be released from the hospital and transferred to the hospice the same day Mason was born. They rearranged his discharge for the following day so that I could have some time to deal with the loss of Mason after he was delivered. I had gone to Harvey's nursing home and packed up everything the day before on Sunday and I packed my van with items that I knew would make Harvey feel more comfortable in transitioning from the nursing home to the hospice. I brought his robe and slippers that my sister Stephanie had given him, one of his throw blankets, his war and military books, other reading materials, his toiletries, and familiar photographs to the hospice. I put his items away and tried to make his room seem more like home.

CHAPTER TEN

Yvette was discharged from the hospital on Tuesday, December 17, 2013. It was an extremely saddening and difficult day. I parked my van in front of the hospital and obtained approval from the valet department to leave it there until Yvette and Jesse were picked up. I went up to the room and when I entered Jesse and Yvette were packing up their personal items, baby molds, and the wooden dragonfly box with some of Mason's items. We packed a cart with their belongings and the nurse brought a wheelchair to transport Yvette to the entrance of the hospital. Jesse pushed the cart with all the items from their stay at the hospital, including Mason's diaper bag, clothes, blankets, and Mason's feather.

It was distressing, sad, and devastating to walk them out of the hospital without their bundle of joy. What an enormous loss of a sweet soul. What heart-wrenching pain we all endured.

When we left the hospital I drove to Miller Funeral Home to discuss the final arrangements for Mason. Jesse, Yvette, and I met with Brian, a director and we discussed the expenses that were above and beyond so that we knew what to expect financially. We provided the director with information for Mason's obituary and we all viewed a final draft before it was published. After the obituary was completed, the director talked to us about the manner of how we wanted Mason taken care of. We told him that we wanted Mason to have a proper burial. The director was kind to notify us that the coffins were on the other side of the curtain he was going to open. The director explained to us that there were two different kinds of infant caskets. One was biodegradable and the other had a vault built into the coffin. I was shocked to see the infant coffins. They were tiny and at first didn't appear to be very

41

sturdy. It wasn't what I expected at all. I looked at Jesse when we were viewing the coffins after the funeral director explained that one was biodegradable. He looked upset so we discussed it and I asked the funeral director if there were any more coffins and he said there were. We walked to the other side of the room and the director once again warned us before opening the curtain. There on the wall behind the curtain was a display of infant and children's coffins. We chose a baby light blue coffin that had a built-in vault. I could see that that selection provided both Jesse and Yvette with some comfort and solace, knowing their baby boy was going to be protected from the elements and may also be moved to be buried next to them later when they make their own final arrangements. Miller told us about a foundation that often assists families with burial expenses related to a baby or a child.

After finalizing the arrangements for Mason's funeral I took Jesse and Yvette to her grandmother's home so they could be around her family and prepare the food for the wake the next day.

They weren't feeling up to going with me to select the flowers for Mason's funeral so I traveled to the Flower Mill to pick out flowers for Mason's casket. I looked through their catalogs and took a picture of a spray I thought that Jesse and Yvette might like. I sent them a picture and they both told me that they liked it. I ordered the flower spray for Mason's casket and I also selected a statue with an eagle soaring high above the mountains and on it included an engraved scripture:

Those who hope in the Lord *will renew their strength. They will soar on wings like eagles.*

Isaiah 40:31

We gave that statue to Jesse and Yvette as a remembrance and to remind them that if they have hope in the Lord their strength will be renewed.

After the flowers were selected, I went to a store called Achieve now known as Lifescape. Lifescape is a store that carries jewelry that is made by people who have special needs. Lifescape promotes these individuals' abilities. Since my son Brian was born with Down syndrome I have been familiar with the store for some time and thought it would be a good time to go and see if they had any dragonfly jewelry.

The customer service person was very helpful. I found a dragonfly necklace for Jesse and Yvette. I also found dragonfly charms for Yvette's grandmother, Yvonne, Yvette's dad, Lorenzo, Yvette's mom, Marlene – and one for myself for my Pandora bracelet.

I felt by giving Jesse, Yvette, and Yvette's family members a dragonfly it was a small, but significant gesture to honor Mason. It is a trinket we each have that makes us think of Mason when we look at them. Lorenzo was grateful for the gesture and he thanked me for the dragonfly a couple of times.

CHAPTER ELEVEN

Harvey was released from the hospital and transferred to hospice the same day Yvette was released from the hospital. Harvey's sister Helen agreed to be at the hospice for his arrival.

After I had finished planning for Mason's funeral, I stopped by to check on Harvey before I left for home. He looked comfy and completely at home. He was surprised to see some of his personal items already there and organized.

His eyes looked sad when he looked at me as I know that he was sad for my loss. He asked me how everyone was and I gave him an update. He told me how sorry he was to hear about Mason. He told me to drive carefully on the way home, as he always did.

It gave me some piece of mind to see that he appeared to be adjusting well.

CHAPTER TWELVE

Our families were instructed to arrive at the funeral home at 3:00 p.m. to gather and have an opportunity to see Mason before the wake. We arrived and Jesse and Yvette went to say goodbye to their son. After they had spent some time with him alone, Yvette's mother Marlene and I went and said our own goodbyes. He was in a baby blue outfit with a teddy bear on his shirt and a hat. He was wrapped in a knitted prayer shawl and covered with his christening blanket. He was beautiful and to me, he looked like an angel. I kissed his forehead and I said my good-byes. I was having trouble catching my breath so I stepped out for a while to get some fresh air. I stood outside and cried, took some slow deep breaths and went back inside.

The funeral director gave us some instructions, and Jesse and Yvette decided the casket would remain open for the wake, but it would be closed for the funeral as they would be leaving the church immediately following the funeral to go to the cemetery and his casket with the built-in vault had to be sealed before the burial.

We had the wake for Mason at Calvary Episcopal Cathedral from 5:00 p.m. to 9:00 p.m. By the time I arrived my friend Marti had all the food assembled and ready. I didn't expect that at all. We have been friends since we were quite young. Marti had been a blessing during this time and, although she had many of her own struggles, she remained steadfast and true.

The wake was a combination of Native American tradition and Christianity. Yvette's father and some of his friends came and performed a Native American Death Ritual ceremony for Mason and our families. They sang songs in their native language, played their drum and they said a prayer in

Native American language and in English.

Yvette's hair was braided and her father gave her scissors so that she could cut her braid. This was also a Native tradition. Yvette and Jesse stepped into the other room and Jesse cut off her braid. Yvette gently placed her braid in Mason's coffin.

These are all death rituals that are customary for some Native American cultures. These ancient death rituals were passed down from their ancestors and are based on their religious beliefs, spiritual beliefs, and life after death. The purpose of these rituals is to guide, comfort, and assist the deceased person with the adjustments to the afterlife.

Yvette's family provided the food for the wake. I was impressed. They had sandwiches, fry bread, various salads, cakes, and punch. It was quite a selection and there was more than enough food.

CHAPTER THIRTEEN

Since the early 1900's, the Lakota Sioux have made Star Quilts. They are presented and used in ceremonies for those who are alive and to cover the casket during a funeral when someone passes away.

This quilt was given to Jesse and Yvette by Yvette's father, Lorenzo. Mason's quilt was laid on top of his casket during the funeral.

It is a tradition for the Dakota and Lakota children to be given quilts throughout their lifetime. Quilts are given at birthdays, graduations, and marriage.

Also, in Lakota tradition, the mourning period after the death of a loved one is a year. Often, at the end of that period, the tribe will hold a special ceremony. The tribesmen, the drummers, singers, pallbearers, family, and friends of the deceased get together for a ceremony. Sometimes Star Quilts are given by some of the family members to people who were involved with the funeral and burial of the deceased.

Giving someone a quilt is significant in that it demonstrates that the person or tribe that has given it to you has a great deal of respect for that person.

Mason's Lakota Star Quilt.

CHAPTER FOURTEEN

The next day was Mason's funeral. Dan and Brian were waiting for me and I had to literally force myself to walk out the door. It was as if I thought that if I didn't show up for the funeral, this really didn't happen.

The church was founded in 1872 and this actual sanctuary was built in 1889. It was the first church built in the city of Sioux Falls, South Dakota. It was a beautiful church constructed with the architectural style of gothic revival. The Very Reverend Ward Simpson told me that Calvary Episcopal Cathedral is a smaller example of what is known as, "Richardsonian Romanesque" architecture and the exterior of the building was made with local Sioux Quartzite stone. Construction was started in late 1888 and completed in late 1889. Thus last year marked the 125th year of the building. What a beautiful church it is, inside and out.

This church also houses "The Teddy Bear Den", which is like a store that women can go to and utilize points they have accumulated during their pregnancy for making good healthy choices and these young women can purchase baby items with these points. It is a program that has helped thousands of young women.

I made it to the church right before the funeral started. I held it together until I saw my foster brother Dave. I went over to him and gave and got a hug and I burst out crying.

None of my other siblings showed up. That too was disheartening. My brother Mark wasn't able to get off of work.

The funeral was a combination of Native American tradition and Christianity. It was a beautiful service and it represented both of our families' faiths and traditions. While listening to the prayers said in native language, although I didn't understand what was being said, it was spiritual, touching, and sad.

I watched Jesse and Yvette consoling each other trying to get through the day they had to lay their beautiful son to rest.

Yvette's father Lorenzo had some tribal members come to the funeral. Most of them had been at Yvette's hospital room previously. Yvette's father burnt white sage in the church and fanned the smoke towards each person in the church. The tribal men sat in a drum/singing circle and they began to sing, play the funeral drum, and chant.

I contacted an old friend of mine. We used to work together as limousine drivers for numerous years and he also has a great voice and sings for weddings and funerals. He wasn't able to sing at the funeral as he had to work. He went out of his way and found a soloist who was able to sing at Mason's funeral. Carol sang, "The Wind Beneath My Wings", and she sang it beautifully.

When we were arranging the plans for the funeral, I asked Yvette if any of her family members would be able to recite a poem or scripture during the ceremony. Yvette told me that all of her family members were shy and she didn't think they would be able to do it.

I asked a dear friend of mine, Vicki, to read scripture from the Book of Isaiah, Isaiah 66:7-14. She read it beautifully.

Another dear family friend, Becca, read the poem that my daughter Brandy had sent. The author of the poem was unknown:

> *God saw you getting tired,*
> *A cure not meant to be.*
> *So he put his arms around you*
> *And whispered, "Come with me."*
>
> *With tearful eyes we watched you*
> *And saw you fade away,*
> *And although we loved you dearly,*

We could not make you stay.

A golden heart stopped beating,
Your tender hands at rest.
God took you home to prove to us
He only takes the best.

Another friend of our family, who lives on the east coast, designed the cover for the program for Mason's funeral. She wasn't able to make it to Mason's funeral, but she also graciously offered to order and purchase the food for the luncheon after the church service.

As I was having such trouble making myself leave the house that day to go to Mason's funeral service, I called Marti and I told her I was having trouble. I asked Marti if she was willing to pick up the food for the luncheon for me and she didn't hesitate. My mom picked up and paid for the cake I pre-ordered that said, "We Love You" and it had a beautiful blue dragonfly.

I am so thankful for my friends always, but I was particularly thankful that none one of them hesitated to help when I reached out to them.

CHAPTER FIFTEEN

It was a bitter, cold, bone-chilling, brisk day. The temperature was in the single digits. Mind you, this was in the middle of December in South Dakota.

After Mason's funeral, we went to the cemetery for his burial. My husband Dan and my son Brian stayed in the van due to the frigid temperatures. I pulled the van up close enough so they could see the burial site.

My uncle Mike, my ex-husband Rich, and Yvette's dad Lorenzo were the pallbearers. Yvette's father's friends sang and played their drum while Mason's casket was lowered in to the ground. A tractor pulled up with a load of dirt and we were given the option to shovel dirt on top of Mason's casket. Some of our family members and the tribal members partook in this tradition.

A prayer was said and Mason's burial was completed. As people left and returned to their vehicles, I stood back for a while and watched Jesse and Yvette comfort each other. I went back to my van and looked over towards Mason's grave and Jesse and Yvette stood out in the cold together, hovering over their son's grave. It was distressing and unbearable to watch. Although it was bitter cold they both stood there and lingered as if they didn't want to leave Mason. It was an extremely saddening day.

We returned to the church for the luncheon. I prepared plates for Daniel, Brian, and myself and then I returned to cut the cake. I stood there at the table, cutting the cake and placing them on the plates while a friend of Yvette's grandmother passed them out to the guests at the funeral. My foster mom Liz came over to me and told me I should sit down. I felt dazed and lost. I stood there and continued cutting the cake until it was completely done. It was exactly enough pieces of cake for everyone down to the last person. I couldn't help but realize that and I found it kind of amazing.

I sat down with my family and a few of my dear friends and I ate some food. My foster mom offered to take Daniel and Brian home as it is physically draining for Daniel to be away from home for very long. Liz took them home and I stayed at the church and finalized a few things.

Rich and his wife Sharon reimbursed us for half of the expenses. It was comforting to know that they were also there for our son and Yvette.

It had been a very unique and personal funeral for my grandson and it was healing.

Jesse and Yvette rode to Yvette's grandmother's home with his dad and Sharon and I took some of Yvette's relatives to Yvette's grandmother's home after we were done at the church. I started to drive home. I cried all the way home with tears streaming down my face.

CHAPTER SIXTEEN

Four days after Mason passed away, I felt compelled to drive by Sanford USD Medical Center. I recalled one of the tribesmen had said that Mason's spirit would be here for four days and then it would be carried off by an eagle. I slowly drove by the hospital and peered towards the hospital wing where Yvette had delivered Mason. I don't know why I felt so compelled to go there other than for a short time I did feel like I was closer to him.

For most of the next five days following Mason's funeral, I laid in bed the majority of the time and ate chocolate and fudge. I would wake up in the morning and get Daniel and Brian breakfast and I would lie back down. I would get up and start the dishes until I got so dizzy and light-headed that I had to lie down.

Around lunchtime, I would get lunch prepared for Daniel and Brian and I would take it down to them while they were spending time together in the family room.

I would go back to bed and lie down again. I did the same with each meal for my family, but most of the time when I was upright I felt nauseous, dizzy, and light-headed. I had a blood-pressure machine to monitor my blood pressure if needed and when I had these symptoms I would occasionally check my blood pressure and it was only slightly elevated.

The pain that I felt was heart wrenching and at times I cried so hard I wailed. It was a deep, cutting pain and at times I felt as though my heart were breaking.

As the week proceeded I continued to do what I could every day, but I was physically and mentally exhausted and depressed. I didn't feel like I had anything left to give.

I started having chest pains in addition to the other symptoms I was having so I decided to go to the acute care and get checked out. I was afraid I was having a heart attack. The doctor ordered a chest x-ray, EKG, and blood work. Everything came back within normal limits. He believed I was experiencing these physical and mental symptoms due to stress.

I realized that I had not been taking care of myself and that I had no choice but to start as I couldn't keep going on like this. I felt like I was so fragile and that I was going to crack or break.

It seemed as though I was getting through the days minute by minute, and then one day at a time. Sometimes without any notice at all, I felt an overwhelming sense of sadness and I just burst out crying. I allowed myself to experience the sadness and cry and grieve. I have found that it is better for my health to face it than to keep it bottled up inside.

I was off work for quite some time as I couldn't concentrate. I felt physically ill, emotionally drained, and exhausted. I slept more and I tried to increase my activity level each day so that I could get back to life and continue to move forward.

CHAPTER SEVENTEEN

Jesse and Yvette called me at midnight on January 1, 2014 and when I saw his picture on my caller ID it made me smile. We had a great talk and he and Yvette were at home celebrating the New Year and they sounded as though they were in good spirits. We talked about how they had both been; we had a few laughs and the fact that he would think about me right at midnight on New Year's made me smile.

Jesse has been calling me more often since Mason has passed away and that is one positive thing that has happened. The loss of our little man has brought us all closer together.

The second thing that I have found to be positive since we lost Mason is that I have realized that I need to start taking care of myself. That was a wake-up call.

I have been a mother for 34 years and I had never really taken care of myself. Now it was time. I put a plan into place and I started executing it and it made getting through each day a little easier as I have been keeping busy and I have been productive.

I have been on the back burner for way too long and I could not continue living my life that way.

Third, my mom has also been very attentive and calling me to check on me, and trying to get me to go out for dinner. I can tell she has been concerned about me. The last few times I have seen her she says I look like I am tired. I think it is more likely due to the tears I have shed every day for the last month.

My foster mom had been in touch frequently, checking on us to make sure we have everything we need.

My mother-in-law has been there to help with Dan and Brian at times and this also brought our family closer together.

For the first time in our lives we are all being mother-henned and we are grateful for their love, care, and concern.

CHAPTER EIGHTEEN

I had the opportunity to meet the Deacon, Harold Pardew, who started the Angel Lee Cronen Memorial Fund of South Dakota. We met for coffee and a latte at a local coffee shop. I had previously contacted the cemetery and the funeral home to follow up with them regarding Mason's steel marker for his gravesite which still hadn't been placed on his grave. Miller Funeral Home provided Mr. Pardew with my contact information and he called me to schedule a meeting to discuss my grandson's headstone.

Mr. Pardew provided me with the history and explanation for the reason that he created the Angel Lee Cronen Memorial Fund of South Dakota. A long time ago, he had met a young woman whose baby passed away when she was only twenty weeks pregnant. The young lady didn't have the funds for a proper burial and the only other option this young woman had would be to have the hospital take care of the baby. According to Deacon Pardew and the hospital, the baby would be disposed of in the same way the hospital would dispose of chemical waste. Angel Lee's mother really wanted a proper burial for her daughter, so Deacon Pardew paid for her daughter's funeral. After that Deacon Pardew was inspired to create a memorial fund in honor of this young woman's daughter, Angel Lee Cronen, thus creating the Angel Lee Cronen Memorial Fund of South Dakota. Deacon Pardew raises funds and obtains donations in an effort to provide this financial assistance to families during the most difficult time in their lives, the loss of an infant or child. Since this memorial fund was implemented, Deacon Pardew has helped over 100 families in one way or another to assist them financially so their deceased baby or child may have a proper burial.

Mr. Pardew was very kind and compassionate during

our conversation. He said that his fund would be willing to pay for Mason's headstone at the cemetery. We talked about our loss, our wishes, and he obtained the information he needed to provide to the family monument company who donates their services.

I was so grateful for this memorial fund's generosity. They had also previously paid for Mason's casket. I was so touched by this man and the organization he created that I decided that I would like to be involved with this memorial fund in one way or another. I told Deacon Pardew that I was interested in being involved with his organization, but I wasn't sure how. He said he would think about that and keep it in mind. Maybe writing this book and glorifying his memorial fund is one way that I can give back to such an empathetic and compassionate organization that was created to lighten the hearts and financial burdens for grieving parents and grandparents.

Mason's headstone was placed on his grave the following spring. We had a dragonfly added to the stone.

CHAPTER NINETEEN

Jesse was my biggest baby at 8 lbs. 15 oz. and 20 ¼ inches long. When he was growing up he was short and stocky until he reached four years old and then he started growing taller and thinned out. He is now 6 ft. 3 inches tall with a medium build.

After Mason was born I realized that I had never seen a baby's foot that size and thought, whoa, he has big feet. The picture of Mason's ultrasound says it all! Look at his foot in comparison to his head!

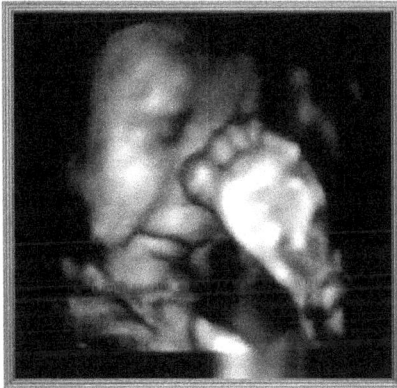

I believe that if Mason had made it to his original due date of January 4, 2014, he would have weighed closer to nine pounds and when fully grown would have reached at least 6'4" in height. He would have been a strong, big, beautiful man with a heart as huge as his daddy's.

Oh, how I wish I would have had the pleasure and opportunity to cuddle you, play with you, teach you about God, faith, love, and life, watch you grow and love you! I won't get any more opportunities to cuddle you while I am here on earth, but I will always love you and I could never ever forget you!

CHAPTER TWENTY

One month after Mason passed away, I had contacted my grandson Brendan's mom, Darla, and I arranged to pick him up. We traveled to Mitchell so that he could spend some time with his dad, Jesse. We hadn't seen Brendan since Mason passed away.

Brendan and I had a great conversation while we were traveling. Brendan told me about the trilogy of movies he intends to produce when he grows up. He has been pretty adamant lately about wanting to be a movie producer. Mitchell is nearly 70 miles away and that was the gist of the majority of our conversation.

I would occasionally look at Brendan in the rear view mirror and sometimes we would lock eyes. Brendan would say, "I love you Grandma. I would say, "I love you more". How precious those moments were. He sure tugs at my heartstrings.

When we arrived at my son's house, we picked him up and went to do some shopping as we didn't see Brendan at Christmas. It was kind of nice doing it this way as he actually got to pick out what he wanted. He was pretty excited and grateful.

We picked up some pizza and went back to Jesse's apartment and ate lunch. After we finished eating, Brendan started putting together some of his Legos. He and his dad played with them for a while after they were assembled.

Brendan also loaded Marvel, one of his new games for his Nintendo 3DS. The look on his face while he was playing his new game was priceless. The concentration and the different facial expressions were quite entertaining. I could tell he was enjoying his new Christmas presents.

Brendan noticed Mason's quilt as it was hanging on his

dad's bedroom wall. We told Brendan that it was Mason's. He proceeded to tell his dad and me what the different colors in the quilt meant. I was so impressed. That was about the coolest thing ever. Brendan truly was absorbed and knowledgeable in his heritage in many aspects.

I hadn't realized that the colors in the quilt had such significance and symbolism. The red in Mason's quilt symbolized birth, faith, beauty, and happiness; the black symbolized maturity, strength, victory, or success; the yellow symbolized intellect, determination, or death; the white symbolized mourning, sharing, purity, and light. The white color may also be used as a symbolism representing peace and happiness; and the color blue symbolize wisdom, intuition, and confidence. These colors may also have different meanings depending on the Native American culture. Color symbolisms may vary between cultures and whether the colors are used for face paint, war paint, or for symbols.

During our day with Brendan, he also told me that he wanted to learn to speak Crow. His great-grandmother, who is a very wise and beautiful Crow Native, is fluent in that language. Since Brendan's great-grandmother lives with him and his mother, I told Brendan to ask her every day how to say a new word and he would be able to increase his knowledge of that language in no time at all. He seemed to think that was a pretty good idea.

After I took Brendan back home, I drove away and cried. It made me realize how blessed that I was to still have Brendan. I thanked God for my sweet, loving, compassionate, smart, and handsome grandson. It makes me realize that although we lost Mason, there are good things to come yet in this life and I am going to do the best I can to have faith and determine what path the Lord wants me to take in moving forward. At least I am starting to have glimmers of peace and hope that this life has more wonderful events and memories ahead. Mason would want me to make the best of it. He would want us to live, laugh, and most importantly he would want us to love each other. I am appreciating the simple things more than ever and I am starting to look forward towards the future and I hope there are many more great memories we will be able to create as a family. Although Mason won't be with us physically, he will always be with us spiritually and in our hearts. Mason will never be forgotten.

CHAPTER TWENTY-ONE

It took forty-two long, agonizing days after we lost Mason before Yvette received the autopsy results. I had called her and she told me that the results weren't definitive. They told us at the hospital that sometimes the autopsy doesn't reveal the exact cause of death, which was the case here. Yvette's grandmother was a nurse and she looked at the autopsy report and didn't really understand it. Yvette asked me if I would come with her to her doctor appointment the following week. I said I would.

Receiving this news from Yvette was so difficult to hear and I felt like I regressed in my grieving process. I lay in bed for hours and cried, wondering why. Wondering if it had been the umbilical cord, the blood clot that they found in Yvette's placenta? Why? What happened to our Mason?

The following week, I went with Yvette to her doctor appointment.

While we were waiting, Yvette gave me a copy of the autopsy report. I read through the six-page report. Due to my employment background and my college education, I do understand a lot of medical terminology. It was a lengthy, thorough report.

We had to wait a considerable amount of time in the waiting room. Yvette and I discussed our feelings about the loss of Mason and she said that when she went to the doctor the first time, after Mason passed away, the waiting room at the clinic was filled with babies and children. She said that everywhere she looked there was a reminder that she had lost Mason. It consumed her so much she told me that she felt like screaming.

I told her I had been going through the same thing and how I don't know when to expect it. I can be in a store, driving down the road, or someone can ask me a question, and without any notice at all, I start crying.

We talked about the stages of grief and how we need to experience it and not internalize it and cover it up as it wouldn't lead to a healthy outcome.

I asked Yvette if she would go to her counselor as she had not seen her since Mason passed away. Yvette said she would. Yvette said her dad also asked her if she would make an appointment. Lorenzo and I seemed to be on the same page in a lot of instances.

Jesse had to work and he lives a distance away, so we called Jesse so that he could be present at the doctor appointment telephonically. I dialed his number and placed him on speaker so that he could hear the doctor discuss the results of Mason's autopsy. Yvette's doctor confirmed that the autopsy was not definitive as to the cause of Mason's death. It could have been the umbilical cord or blood clots in the placenta. If that is the case, the doctor said that if Yvette plans to have more children she would be monitored for the blood clots so that if there were blood clots in the placenta they can be prevented next time. When Yvette decides to have more children, her pregnancy would be considered high-risk due to the loss of Mason.

The doctor said that Mason may have passed away due to the umbilical cord being kinked for too long a time, or it could have been that the umbilical cord got wrapped around Mason's foot and he struggled to get it loose and the umbilical cord was tight for too long cutting off Mason's oxygen. It took Yvette back to the night before Mason's heart quit beating when she was awakened from a deep sleep with a sharp stabbing pain. Now it makes Yvette wonder if that is when her Mason passed away.

The doctor also asked Yvette if she had seen her counselor since Mason passed away and Yvette confirmed she had not. Yvette's doctor suggested that she schedule an appointment.

I was concerned about Yvette as she was unemployed and living with her grandmother and numerous other relatives. She doesn't have many opportunities to be by herself and although I didn't want her alone for very long, it may help if she was able to have a little time to herself to properly grieve.

Jesse and Yvette have had difficulty dealing with the loss of Mason and then learn there is no definitive cause. It had dredged up a lot of emotions and doubt and it has not provided them with any peace of mind, not knowing or understanding why their son was gone.

They went through a stage of somewhat questioning each other and blaming each other. I told them that they can't do that to each other as the mere suggestion is very hurtful and it isn't something you can take back. I told them both that it wasn't either of their faults and no one knows what happened, except God. I told them I don't understand why we had to lose him either, but Mason wouldn't want them to blame each other. Mason wouldn't want them to fight and they needed to make steps to move forward and in doing so, whatever they decided to do they need to honor their son and honor his memory.

CHAPTER TWENTY-TWO

Jesse and Yvette have Mason's hand and foot molds and his hand and foot prints from the hospital; Mason's Star Quilt; and Mason's feather.

After my foster mom Liz Bowling painted the book cover for this book, she made a picture for Jesse and she matted and framed it so that he could always have that to remember Mason!

Also, a dear friend of mine touched up a photograph of my grandson Mason so that it looked as though he was sleeping! That meant a great deal to Jesse, Yvette and me.

Some people may not understand why they have kept some of these things, but besides their memory of their infant son Mason, the pictures of him, his foot and hand molds and the star quilt are the only things they have left of him.

Almost two months after Mason passed away, Jesse and Yvette decided to post some pictures of Mason on their Facebook. There were a few complaints stating, "graphic violence". Jesse and Yvette were really upset.

They don't get to watch Mason grow up. They don't get to watch him make milestones. These mementoes are all they have left of Mason besides the love they feel for him in their hearts and souls. They didn't post them to offend anyone. They didn't post them to be grotesque or morbid. They posted their pictures of their son as he was beautiful, and they wanted people to see that beauty. They are forever changed due to Mason's existence and his passing. This is their way of grieving. Who is anyone to tell them how to grieve? This is the path that only they know how to travel and to get through each day. They do whatever they have to, to survive without their beautiful son, Mason.

Thankfully, Facebook found in their favor and they were

able to have their pictures posted.

Not too many people probably understand where we are coming from and how tight we want to hold on to everything that reminds us of our precious Mason. It is an emotional attachment to our broken hearts and that is the only other way I can describe it.

We will never ever forget that Mason was here. We will never ever forget that Mason touched our hearts. We will never ever forget that Mason's very existence has changed us all forever.

CHAPTER TWENTY-THREE

After sustaining the tragic loss in our family, I found writing my journal notes, which evolved into writing this book, helped me deal with the grief that I have endured as the result of the loss of my second grandchild Mason and witnessing the pain and agony Jesse and Yvette went through during his passing. I was only Mason's grandmother, but Jesse and Yvette were his parents and I knew the pain I experienced. I can't imagine the pain that they both have gone through.

I started out journaling during this extremely difficult time in our lives as I felt I had to express myself and I had to get my feelings out. I found writing to be therapeutic and healing and my journal notes were transformed into this book. I felt compelled to write about this tragic senseless loss that will forever remain an unknown mystery and to let people know about this testimony of how I have survived with God's strength and faithfulness. When we lost Mason, I had no idea what to do, how to react, or how to properly grieve. As painful as this has been, we knew we had to go through the stages of grief and face it head on as we couldn't deny what we witnessed and we have had no choice but to face it. I had to be strong for my son Jesse and his girlfriend Yvette. We had to immerse ourselves in this grief and we have all been completely absorbed by it, while the rest of the world appears to go on without missing a beat. We had to let ourselves feel what we needed to feel and do what we needed to do each moment of the day to continue through life and to not only survive, but hopefully thrive.

Initially, I was angry with God, but then someone told me that God didn't do this. That God wouldn't have taken the life of this precious child and I knew I couldn't stay mad at Him as my faith and reliance in the Lord was and is the only way I was going to survive this loss. He has carried us through this difficult time. They say God won't give you more than you can handle, but I think God gives you the strength to endure whatever it is you are faced with. As long as you remain faithful and give it back to God, he will give you what you need to get through those times.

I am positive that I would not have been able to survive the loss of my grandson Mason Warren if it were not for my faith. I prayed each step of the way and asked God to give me the strength to do what I needed to do to get through this tragic loss, to give me enough strength to be there for my son and Yvette and to do what I needed to do. I feel as though this testament of what the Lord did for our family during this time should also be told and be witness to the love, strength, and compassion we receive from the Lord when we are faithful.

As time has passed I have visited Mason's grave on numerous occasions and sometimes I take things to his grave, sometimes I light a candle in his honor and every time I say a prayer for him and I talk to him. So far we have decorated his plot with flowers, candles, spinners, Christmas decorations and Teddy Bears on Valentine's Day and every other holiday that comes our way. I will continue to do this for the rest of my life and in some ways it does make me feel closer to him when I am there.

I have noticed numerous blessings. Most of them are small and as simple as finding a parking spot in the hospital ramp right near the door to the floor of Yvette's hospital room. The day after I went to the funeral home and had returned to the hospital, the parking ramp was full. I drove around the ramp from level to level and as I was reaching the skywalk floor which was the easiest way to get to Yvette's room, a couple got into their van and they were parked right by the door. I smiled and looked up and thanked God. It may seem trivial to you, but I had such an exhausting day and being able to park right by the entrance provided me with some relief considering the circumstances and it was a blessing. Some of them have been major blessings wrapped in big lessons, such as realizing that something I had searched for all of my life was there for me all the time.

Self-employment has provided me with the flexibility to take care of my family and in some cases, work around their schedules. It has truly been a blessing and with the way our life has been in the last three years, I don't know that I would have been able to maintain a position of employment with a typical law firm, especially considering the time I have taken off of work since Mason passed away, in order to prepare for his wake, funeral, and to grieve.

I have learned so many lessons since Mason passed away, from realizing I have to take care of myself; setting boundaries in my life; re-prioritizing my life; letting go of some of the people in my life who are toxic to me and my family; writing about my grief and getting it all out; and the fact that I surprised myself with the strength I have in Christ. This has been a very difficult journey, yet liberating. I have realized that I cannot continue to seek validation from some of the people in my life who aren't able to give it; won't give it or they are just plainly not empathetic or compassionate. I have felt empty. Always giving of myself and not getting anything in return. I don't want to hurt these people's feelings as they have hurt mine, but I am depleted and I just can't keep giving when they obviously don't care about me and my family and the struggles that we have dealt with for the last eleven years. Instead, I have moved on without them, but I do pray for them.

I felt like I was missing something most of my life and I sought for validation and what I thought I was missing from my dad. As part of this process I have also discovered that I don't need validation from anyone anymore as God validates me and that is all I need now.

As time has passed since Mason passed away, Jesse and Yvette's relationship had been more difficult. In the beginning the loss of Mason brought them closer together. Then they continued to be together off and on. I thought that going through something like this, in the end, would either bring them even closer together or tear them apart. In the end, it was actually something else that caused their relationship to end.

I try to remain available for the both of them and occasionally one or the other will call me. I try to be an advocate; a counselor; a mother and a friend to both. I listen to both of them and occasionally offer some advice or make a suggestion. I hope they can continue to remain close so that they can continue to be there for each other through their grief.

We are all still hurting emotionally and physically, but we are trying to continue with our lives even though it will never be the same. Hopefully more blessings will derive from this tragic loss and we want to proceed with life keeping Mason's spirit alive and maybe our loss will help someone else who may find themselves facing such an enormous loss as we have.

CHAPTER TWENTY-FOUR

After Mason had passed away, my husband gave me a trip to Florida for my Christmas present. I had planned that trip to meet a friend of mine from Virginia, but before I had a chance to go, my step-dad Harvey passed away. It was on Valentine's Day, exactly two months after Mason died.

I had considered canceling my trip, but I knew if I didn't go Harvey would have been disappointed. I decided that I was going to go because I KNEW he would want me to. I met my dear friend for a three-day weekend. It was a much-needed trip for both of us due to various events that were occurring in our lives. When we arrived at our hotel and went down to the restaurant for dinner, I told her that I think we both needed to talk and vent about some of the things we had going on so we could get it all out and enjoy our trip. Amazingly enough we spent a lot less time venting than I thought that we would. Then I said, "Ok we are done now. Let's enjoy the rest of our trip".

The second day of our trip we went kayaking in the ocean in Sarasota, Florida. We kayaked through three separate mangrove tunnels, and we saw herrings flopping out of the water, herons, upside down jellyfish and we saw and I held a sea urchin. It was a great trip. The next morning we went outside of our hotel for dolphin watching. Our hotel was located right on the Gulf of Mexico. We had been dolphin watching for some time and within five minutes of my friend returning to our room to retrieve something, I saw and videoed two dolphins swimming in front of our hotel. It was unbelievable!

It was a short trip and I didn't want to go home. That was the first time I went somewhere and actually didn't want to go back home.

Once I returned from my vacation, I told my husband that I hadn't wanted to come home. I think he kind of took it personally until I showed him all the beautiful pictures that I took while I was gone and he told me he understood completely why I didn't want to come home.

Although it was only a long weekend, it felt great to get away and it provided me with some respite and rejuvenation to return home to life and all of my responsibilities. It was amazing what a weekend get-a-way did for my disposition.

CHAPTER TWENTY-FIVE

The following July after Mason's passing, Brian and I attended the Joy Ranch's "We Get It Camp". Joy Ranch is a facility wherein the property was donated by an amazing woman, Joy Nelson. This was the third year in a row that we attended this summer camp. It is special in the way that it is an amazing 1880's - looking town that contains modern amenities and has family retreats. A couple that run this facility through Lutheran Outdoors, Kyle and Betsy Debertin, the staff and the families we have met over the last three years truly do get it.

We checked in at the Thirsty Boot Saloon and we were assigned room number 7. Each room has a theme. When we got to our room, I opened the door and on the wall behind the beds were two star quilts. There was a document on the wall titled, "Star Quilt", and it contained the Dakota/Lakota history of Star Quilts. I lost it again, and I broke down crying. I walked outside and the plaque on the wall said Star Quilt Room. The pictures in our room were painted by my two favorite artists - Oscar Howe and JoAnn Bird. I was astounded. It is amazing how God works.

As Yvette had Mason's quilt, I asked my aunt Karen to make Mason's quilt for Jesse so he could always have it. My aunt Karen did duplicate Mason's quilt for Jesse and she made one for me too. They are forever keepsakes and they were made with many prayers and love.

Since Mason passed away, Yvette and Jesse have both had dreams with Mason included. Yvette told me that in her dream Mason told her that he was ok and that he wanted her to be happy.

Now, we all notice dragonflies, Jesse, Yvette and I. One day Yvette was swarmed by them and it kind of startled her.

Now, when Yvette, Jesse and I see dragonflies all we can

do is think of Mason. Yvette believes the dragonflies are Mason, coming to her to let her know that he is ok.

A year to the day that we lost Mason; there was a candlelight service that was held at Westminster Presbyterian Church. We made arrangements to meet at Mason's grave before attending the candlelight service. I arrived at the cemetery and Jesse and Yvette were there with a few others. While I was there Yvette's mom stopped and gave Yvette a hug and she shook my hand before leaving and walking away with tears in her eyes. I was told that Yvette's father had been there before I arrived and he had left as he was not feeling well. I had brought a wreath that I decorated at home and placed it on a stand. I gave it to Jesse and he placed it at Mason's gravesite. I said a prayer and gave Yvette and Jesse a hug before I left. Later that evening we met at the church and attended the memorial for Mason. A friend of mine told me about it. The service was beautiful and it was very difficult for Jesse. I found myself being strong for him until the song "Precious Child" began and I lost it. I was no longer able to be strong enough for myself, let alone Jesse. Such a precious child Mason was.

December 16, 2014 was exactly one year since Mason was delivered. Yvette called me and asked if I would come over to her house so that we could release lanterns for Mason. I went over and we all drove together to her cousin's home, Nate and Kristeen. Kristeen had graciously made dinner and fry bread for everyone and after everyone ate, we assembled the lanterns and walked across the street to a big open field while Yvette and I lit lanterns for Mason and Kristeen lit a lantern for her grandmother. It was amazing to watch our lanterns lift off into the sky until they were little dots and they would disappear. Jesse was unable to come due to work, but I took pictures and video so that he could see it all.

We are all still trying every day to put one foot in front of the other although, sometimes each of us has wanted to give up. I keep reminding myself, Jesse, and Yvette that we can't give up. We need to move forward and try and honor Mason with what we choose to do for the rest of our lives and that someday when our time has come, we will be with Mason again for eternity.

AFTERWORD

If you or anyone you know loses a child and lives in South Dakota, contact Angel Lee Cronen Memorial Fund of South Dakota. Also, if you are looking for a worthy organization to contribute funds while you are planning your estate or choosing your annual charity, please consider donating funds to this memorial fund as Deacon Harold Pardew was not only a blessing to our family when we lost Mason, but he has been a blessing to over one hundred families to date.

http://www.sfcatholic.org/dwc/Files/OfficeofRespectLife/PDFs/AngelLeeCronenFund.pdf

Blessings! Pay it forward!

AUTHOR PAGE

Kimberly Wells is a new author and Losing Mason is her first published book. Mrs. Wells does come from a family of writers. Her grandmother Margaret Tidemann wrote her own life story and had a poem, "The Sunflower", published in the Great American Book of Poetry. Her uncle Michael Tidemann is a published author of "Doomsday" and "The Elk and Other Stories".

Kimberly's primary education is in the legal field and she has a Bachelor's Degree in Paralegal Studies. She currently owns and operates her own business, Wells Paralegal & Private Investigator Service. She has worked in the legal field for nineteen years.

Kimberly started writing quite a few years ago, but she wasn't moved to publish anything until the events that occurred as detailed in her first book, Losing Mason. After the loss of Mason she started journaling the events that were taking place in an effort to assist her with the grieving process after this tragic and unthinkable loss. As the journaling continued she felt compelled to turn her journaling notes in to a book. Writing became her therapeutic tool during her walk through grief.

Kimberly is currently working on her second book.